In and Out of My Element

A Poetic Memoir

Gianna Amador Baldazo

Dedication:

To my inner child,
You are beautiful and strong
from the inside out.

Contents

Ignition

I had a heart attack the day he left me ... or that's what it felt like. I locked myself in the bathroom, suffocating, as I breathed in the smoke of a fire I know I started. I didn't want anyone to see me cry over him. I was scared that I would never get over him. I was afraid to live without him. I wanted to rip my heart out of my chest, but he had already done that. He served it to me on a silver platter and suddenly decided to put it back as if he could make me feel alive again.

That's the way gentlemen break hearts. They do it gently.

I could tell we weren't ready when we tried again to mend each other's broken hearts and keep things steady. At first, I blamed him. However, nearly a year later, I'm starting to believe my heartbreak was self-inflicted. From a very young age, I grew up with a rage I camouflaged quite impressively. I've always had a talent for bottling it all in, a little girl carrying around the aftermath of her father's sin. Absence has such a presence. The assumption of in-and-out privileges speaks volumes about the amount of entitlement and selfishness one has. You can't come and go as you please.

This is nothing new to me, but as a young woman, I never expected the same behavior from a man I truly believed to be my soulmate. I was convinced we were made for each other, him and I. I even went as far as defending him when others judged our situation, but he was not the one who needed defending.

The blame is not all on him. It takes two. I got issues, too; issues that are now coming to the forefront of my mind. I have many things I need to work on as I try to move on because it all starts with self-love at the end of the day. I need to work on all the things I've been trying to run away from. I need to work on all the things I haven't healed from yet. When you never get closure, pain and dysfunction follow you no matter how much time has passed. It's hard to love with this bitter taste in my mouth. It tastes a lot like disappointment and confirmation of why I choose to be alone.

It takes a lot of power and strength to love in a world that doesn't love you back. I admire people who love anyway. I wish I could be more like them. They say life is what you make it. I'm starting to wonder if love is what you make it, too. I'm starting to believe that you could choose to love or not love someone. I'm starting to realize that love stays alive when respect, loyalty, honesty, communication, and friendship keep the flame going because love alone is not enough. But no one has the patience these days.

I hope to one day experience genuine love. I hope to one day meet someone who makes me a hopeful romantic. I hope to one day meet someone who inspires me to be better than I was yesterday. I hope to one day meet someone strong enough to stick around when times get tough. I hope to one day meet my best friend—a friendship set on holy fire. I hope one day I'm not intimidated by a new flame, someone pure and out of this world. I hope one day I get to tell my future husband how fine and divine he is. I hope I don't go down in flames before then.

I hope I learn how to love again. I hope I learn the difference between a man who would warm my heart and a man who would watch it burn into ashes.

180 degrees

I am confused, and I lose no matter what I choose.
If you look at every angle, every perspective, nobody wins.
I'm hurt
I'm disappointed
And I'm angry,
With you and myself
With the situation itself.
I never thought you would put me in this position.
I never thought I would ignore my intuition.
Listen—
I'm not a quitter, my love.
I know you know me well enough,
But you don't know me as well as I thought
If you thought that I would be happy
With being "chosen."
I wanted so badly for it to work out
Even if it meant leaving myself
Feeling disrespected and insecure.
I shouldn't have to prove I love you more.
And the more I think about it the more I realize
That we never stood a chance when it came to romance.
It ended before it ever really started
And I'm starting to think you like the attention.
Our love is complicated as it is.
Why did you have to add another dimension?
Why?
Try to see it from my angle.

The truth is...
Nobody will ever be pleased with the outcome of 180 degrees.
The love you claim you have for me doesn't seem to add up.

Falling (in love and apart) ft. Rose Quartz

You left love crystals behind
For me to find
And I find myself collecting new memories of you through
my dreams.
Some nights you were my nightmare.
Some nights you were my relief.
We never rose to the occasion
Or maybe it was just me.
I never understood our situation.
I guess I never really understood
A thing about love.
Ours shattered on the floor, unexpectedly, like those love
crystals did
Right after we made love.
They fell from your wrist.
I kept them, I couldn't resist.
I needed all the love I could get.
I still do.
Love alone is not enough,
Neither were those crystals.
I still miss you.

Next time, I hope falling in love involves bonding by the bonfire, instead of being burned at the stake.

Reasons Why We Were Never Going To Work

1. Our relationship was never clear. I couldn't picture us together in the long run because we were out of focus. And no matter how hard I tried to squint, no matter how hard I tried to adjust the lens, I just couldn't see us achieving our dreams and goals without getting in the way of each other. Lovers need rest. Individuals need to work on themselves and learn themselves— they can only spend the rest of their lives loving others right if they can love themselves first. I don't want to get in the way of your dreams, and I don't want to sacrifice mine. I don't want to leave myself behind.

2. I don't trust you. I don't think I ever did ... simply because you're a man. I can't stand someone who treats me like an option. You had a lot of nerve. I think I've had enough of accepting less than I deserve.

3. You are a gift, but I have to return you. I don't deserve you ... and you don't deserve me.

- I hope you understand.

I don't think anyone deserves me, and there is no one I deserve at this point in time.

Wishful thinking

I sometimes fantasize about one day running into him. God would send that moment as a way of sending him back into my life at the right time and the right place. Being blessed by the smile on his face once again. An opportunity for us to do shit the right way. For us to start over. I'm only human, so I know nothing about God's will for me, obviously. It's wishful thinking. It's not something you should count on or something you can wait for, but a girl can dream, right? Maybe we were never meant to be together, but I'm hoping with time and space to heal ... maybe we can at least be friends.

You Already Know

You never had to ask me to write a poem for you
Never flirtatiously said, *"So where's my poem at?"*
You never had to ask that.
You already knew I wrote a few about you,
Way before we ever had a thing for each other,
Way before we ever owned up to it.
I was in love with you before we ever met.
I was in love with you before I could admit it to my
friends.
I was in love with you before I could admit it to myself.
I was sad to know it had to end
And what breaks my heart is hearing people say
You might have to go through a few heartbreaks until you
find the one.
That really messes with my head.
I can't do this all over again.
I'd rather break a few hearts instead.
I hope one day I never write about you again ...
I will always love you,
But you already know that.

Mere Reflection

I saw my sadness in your eyes the night
We fought temptation,
The night you held me into waterworks,
The night you dove into my eyes and swam in my vulnerability.
I hated that you didn't look away.
I've never had someone willing to venture my lost mind.
I was scared for you,
I was intimidated by your desire to explore me in ways no one ever
had before.
For that I adored you
And wanted more of you.

That night we faced our fears.
That night I was facing a mirror
We were a reflection of each other,
A mere reflection of realization and revelation
Of the shit we needed to change about ourselves.
I wouldn't have been able to realize that with anybody else,
Because we are so much alike.
The male version of me.
I learned a beautiful yet tragic lesson with you
Yet, in so many ways, I still haven't changed.
Was it all a waste?

"We don't need to save
other people. People are capable
of saving themselves."

– A wise soul.

Roaming

I miss him, but I'm afraid to tell him that because I don't know if I'm supposed to. But I do. To know that we roam the same Earth and that he's just an arm stretch away brings heartache to me every day. It killed me at first, but as time passes, it is now a lingering discomfort. A love pain.

Visions and Voicemails

This wasn't supposed to happen, but it did.
I fell in love with The Kid,
But in the process, you lost my trust.
And I lost my best friend.
I haven't felt much since we've parted ways.
I'm sorry I couldn't stay.

I'm a visionary.
It isn't out of the ordinary for me to see into the future sometimes,
Good and bad.
Trust me when I say we wouldn't have been happy.
You trust me, right?
I could have sworn that I warned you
And told you what I needed,
Even though we both knew it wasn't what I wanted.
Neither of us knew what we wanted
At the end of the day—
Every night
You played on my desires.
You broke my heart twice in the matter of a week.
You knew I was weak for you.
Some nights I cry.
Some nights I ask why it had to be you.
Some nights I thank God it was you.
Some nights I write about you
But I never feel satisfied.
Sometimes I want to call you, old friend
Just to hear your voice again.

*I wish I would
chase my dreams
as much as I chase you.*

Soul food

His heartbeat was the harmony of my sad song.
Some days it was cool, calm, and collected.
It put me at ease.
Some nights it was upbeat
For the times we
Anticipated making the kind of love
That everyone would be jealous of.
He loved me so deeply.
He cared for me so deeply.
How did he calm my anxieties yet start a fire in me?
How was I so relaxed, yet hot and bothered in his presence?
I don't even bother trying to figure it out.
Not everything needs an answer.
Not everyone needs a savior.
All I know is his soul was my favorite flavor.

Him.
What a night.
What a sight.

Love/Hate Relationship

I'm about to have my way with you.
I'm about to go all the way with you.
Don't make me choose.
Don't make me lose everything I've been working for.
Stop making me want you more.
Please don't leave me sore and unsure.
Don't make me hate what I adore about you.

April 1, 2018

Do you think you're the only one
I've had to love from a distance?
You're no different.
I no longer bleed over you
I no longer cry over you
I'm over you.
I've been through this
A million times before.
You've hurt me like they have
X 4
This is nothing new to me, but
I'm tired of everyone April foolin' me.

My bad for mistaking
a glare for a halo
... a ghost for an angel.

U and the Sunshine Band

I still feel you in the night time.
I remember you from my past life.
I must've been your wife in the seventies.
It doesn't hurt to think about you as much anymore
But I hate summers now.
The sun just highlights the distance
And the hurt
And the fact that we didn't work out in this lifetime.

I used to think we were so in tune.
I don't listen to the radio anymore;
All I hear is static.
You.
You used to light up my day,
A ray of sunshine,
You used to be mine.
I never got a chance to buy you flowers.
I know how much you love them.
I always appreciated how you stopped to smell the roses.
Getting high, wearing tie dye, such a fly guy.
Old soul, hella retro.

In retrospect, I always respected your perspective.
I would never throw shade.
Because of you I want to buy a pair of those hippie shades.
I should have stolen yours.
If I had them, maybe I wouldn't be so blinded by
Sunny days that don't feel the same.
Although I resent the sun
And how you were not the one for me
I pray you always stay bright.
Don't dim down your light for anybody.
I'll be alright.

Love, Your biggest fan

Archery

I can hide behind the arch in my brows.
I can hide behind the arch in my back.
My pride will prevent me from calling you back.
I'm undecided if I should be proud of that.
I'm looking for an out-of-body experience.
I know deep down you want to experience this.
I know deep down you only want me for my eyebrows.
You love the way they form when I get angry.
I know deep down you get aroused, intellectually.
I know you get turned on, immediately
After I tell you how much you mean to me.
I know you know I love it when you're mean to me.
I love the type of play-fight that leads to making love all
night.
I'm not afraid of love bites.
But I'm afraid you'll never love the real me.
I aim to please
And then I aim to leave.

When Worlds Collide

I'm not quite ready to make eye contact with you yet,
Because I'm not ready to come in contact with the universe
inside you.
You invited me in even as I looked away.
I knew seeing a glimpse of your soul would make me want to
stay.
I didn't want the life in my universe to destroy yours.
I didn't want the life within us to be at war.
You mean more to me than my curiosity to enter your world.
So I stayed away ... for as long as I could.

Love is my favorite language, but I guess I'm not fluent.

Mind Games and Mind Frames

Why do I fall in love with guys
With unique names and mindframes?
Yet I can never picture myself with them forever.
I'm ashamed of my decisions when I choose not to listen,
When I hear what I want to hear
And see what I want to see,
When I'm all up in my feelings.
These men are no good for me.
I can't wait to find the man who's good to me.

We all have people
who we love that we don't
necessarily trust.

– issues

Broke(n)

I have promised myself I will never depend on a man.
I refuse to settle for someone who leaves me empty,
Pockets and soul.
I'm praying for a man with a humble ego,
A man who recognizes a real woman
When he sees one,
Who's unafraid to enter her Queendom.

*I can always depend
on a man to disappoint me.
How disappointing ...*

What a waste ...

Everyone deserves a second chance, but I'm tired of giving a third, fourth, fifth, and sixth chance. There's only so much grace I can give. There's only so much pain I can live with, but I want to see you win. I want to be part of your victory. My superpower and my weakness are that I fall in love with people's potential. I see what they don't see. I forget to realize that I'm in love with a potential they're not using and don't plan on using. Wasted potential. Wasted time. Wasted energy. Wasted love.

He Pulled The Trigger

There have been times
When you have abandoned me
Taken me for granted
Because you knew I would always be there.
You knew I cared.
I do not judge you for this.
We all do this in one way or another
For the security and comfort.
You just got too comfortable.
I just got too comfortable.
And you counted on me to be the understanding person I am
And I gave you the benefit of the doubt.
I doubt that I was even the one.
One moment of neglect
Becomes a trigger.
It is a feeling
One cannot forget.
Even though I'm used to it
It still hurts every time.
But with all the strength inside me
I refuse to hold hands with the fear of abandonment.
I refuse to stay bitter ...
About love.

27

*I know many fallen angels,
but none of them fell quite as
gracefully as you did.*

Everlasting Fire

They say don't play with fire,
But they can't stand the heat like I can.
I understand the fire.
It's my passion.
It's my drive.
It's my desire.
It's everything I aspire to be.
It's my ambition.
It's my goals.
It never dies,
Because it's forever in my soul.
It's the flame within me that keeps me going.
And without me even knowing
Everyone notices,
Because in my eyes the fire is showing.
The only thing I ask of you:
Don't light that match if your spark
Isn't willing to match my flame.
Once it burns out of control
It's hard to maintain.
So when they say don't play with fire,
I guess I understand that, to a certain degree.
It basically means, don't play with me.

Future Fears
and Body Art

As a little girl, I never thought about my future. I never thought about what it would look like or how I wanted it to be. I was never the type of child to play with paper airplanes. I was never the type of girl who fantasized about her wedding day or dream house ... I used to hate when teachers would ask, *Where do you see yourself in five years?* I never knew how to answer that question because I didn't have an answer. I didn't believe I would amount to anything or that I was strong enough to beat the odds against me. Somewhere along the way, I convinced myself it's not worth it to dream big—or to dream at all. I found comfort in my trauma and the pain of the past because it felt familiar. That always stayed the same. Consistent inconsistency. It was all I knew. And the "present time" always seemed to resemble the past more than it did the future.

Anxiety became my best friend. It was always with me, in my past, my present, and my rare attempts to think about the future. Fear of the known and unknown took its toll on my body over the years. My appetite would run, and my heart would race with it. Scars from self-harm became a visual display of a little girl who didn't know what to do when the ground underneath her got a little shaky.

I finally realized I got issues deeper than my own understanding. Deeper than my flesh can fully comprehend. They say the first step to recovery is admitting you have a problem, right? Well, my problem is I'm stuck on step two. I don't know what to do with my newfound issues. Most days, I crave healing with a desire to become the best version of myself. Other days I go back to my old ways. However, I'm starting to notice I'm not afraid anymore. I consider myself a dreamer now. I see myself flying from state to state and making a home out of everywhere I go. I see myself being at peace exploring the world inside my mind.

I want to share it with you through these words if you don't mind.

I've always stayed silent, afraid the wind would carry my words away. I was always afraid no one would care about what I had to say. But now I'm really excited to be heard. I no longer live in my hurt ... or at least I try not to. Because I'm a dreamer, now. I would never have guessed that in my wildest dreams because my wildest dreams used to feed tornados of doubt. My goal now is to make life a breeze from here on out to the best of my ability.

Lost

I lost weight around the same time I lost my mind.
I left my sanity and ten pounds behind.
I put my worries on repeat and rewind.
I wasted time being distracted.
I forgot to put self-care into practice.
I didn't care.
I was unaware of the damage
I was doing to my body.

To let yourself go is a result of holding on
To destructive thoughts, ideas, and attachments.
My mind is a gold mine and I want my body to match it
But all I do is trash it.
Mind, body, and soul,
Help me let go.
I need to get past this.
I was critical instead of constructive.
Mind, body, and soul.
I want to love it all again.
I want to own it all again.
I want to look in the mirror and starve my fears.
I want to look in the mirror
And be proud of all that I've gained
And all that I've lost.
I want to feel like a winner again.

Muscle Memory

Practice makes perfect
Or practice makes petty.
As I work on my goals.
I'm tryna keep things steady.
Old habits I try to forget,
But my mind won't let me.
New habits I try to store
In my brain like data entry.

I have access to it all.
Learning what it feels like
To get up after I fall.
Repetition is the mission.
I should listen to my intuition.
I should listen to my gut.
I should work a little harder.
I should work a little smarter.
I want to master every skill
That's in alignment with God's will.

*Time to bench press the weight of
the world on my chest.
Don't adversity look
sexy on me?*

Management

I can't control my anxiety, but I can try to manage it with
grace.
I'm still learning how to cope with it every day.
The more you try to control it
The more out of control it gets.
I'm still learning how to let go
And how to be in the moment.
When I feel distress coming my way
I have to give myself time
To say it's okay
To feel this way,
But what can I do to alleviate it?

Let's take a deep breath,
In and out.
Breathe until peace comes with every count.
Nobody talks about anxiety, but we all feel it.
Then again, to be anxious about something isn't always nega-
tive.
Sometimes we can be anxious about something exciting.
Although I'm not inviting this overwhelming feeling
I understand it's an everyday battle for me.
Every day is different.
Every day is a mission.
I've been too stubborn to listen,
But I'm starting to realize
Human weakness is an opportunity to showcase human
strength.
When I think about it in that way, I strive to manage it with
grace.

My heart beats rapidly
during catastrophe. It's so
uncomfortable, but it reminds
me that I'm still alive.

Leaves

I write on windy days,
Hoping the breeze will carry me away.
I can't stay.
I need to leave.
I need to breathe.
I need to float.
I need to cope.
I lost all hope.
I lost control.
I'm a light notebook
With heavy emotion.
No wonder I'm still in the same spot.

I rip out each page and let it fly away.
The breeze is my release.
I'll catch my breath
And let the universe handle the rest.
I want to feel light.
I want to be free
Whether or not anyone stays or leaves.

I speak to God on windy days, praying my prayers will reach Him faster, praying He'll free me from this disaster.

Self-fulfilling Scenarios

I thought I was running this whole time,
But I was really jogging in place.
Fear was running this race
And it won.
I dropped the baton.
I got off track.
All I want to do is create
But all I seem to create are scenarios
That keep me in last place.

Why are you afraid
of being great?
Get carried away ...
into greatness

Timer

I fear that life will pass me by. I fear that I'm worrying so much about my ambition and striving for more that I ignore all the blessings right in front of my face. How am I supposed to face that when I'm ninety years old? I'll be telling myself, *"I told you. You should have lived life to the fullest."* I'm so foolish. I'm wasting time. I'm a perfectionist. I wish I could be God's receptionist so I could understand His perfect timing.

Testimony

Investing in yourself is an investment in itself. What works for you may not work for someone else. We all deal with self-doubt. We all deal with stress in different amounts. Sometimes the time and work we put in don't seem to add up. No matter what we have already accomplished, we feel like we aren't enough. Some of us are too hard on ourselves. Keep investing through the stress. Stay blessed and well-rested. Life is a test.

We are not alone.
May that reminder alone
get us through the day

The Art of Being
Broken and Lost

My life is full of frustrated scribbles,
Unfinished sketches,
Resentful splatters of paint,
Insecure typos,
Missing puzzle pieces,
Broken stained-glass windows,
Confusing sculptures,
And storylines with no closure.

You are a work of art.
God put His blood, sweat,
and tears into you.

Racing Thoughts

Thoughts spread like a disease
Or like fire.
Whatever analogy you desire.
Positivity is contagious.
Negativity is dangerous.
Psychologically I owe myself an apology
For believing there was ever something wrong with me.
In all honesty, I've made it this far
With plenty of scars to show how many times I went to war
And how many storms I've endured.
I can see, now, why people pick up a bottle or a blunt.
But even then, some addictions just aren't enough.
I know what it's like to lose track of time.
I know what it's like to lose your mind for an hour or two.
I know what addictions can do to you.
I know what it's like to tell yourself this will be the last time—
One more time until I'm satisfied.
I've cried over the psychological cycle.
I've tried to let my soul take over.
The flesh wants what it wants.
The mind can lead or follow.

Spread Your Wings

You wanna soar,
But your arms are sore.
They're heavy
From the emotions you carry.
You wanna fly
And the last time you felt fly
Was the time
When you truly loved everything about yourself.
Somehow you fell out of love with yourself.
You fell straight out of the sky.

Your wings won't be broken for long.
Soon you'll be strong enough to sing your song.
All you ever needed was you, all along.
I can't wait to watch you spread your wings.

When you spread your wings,
your soul sings.

Marathon

I'm running my own race.
Taking my sweet time,
I grind at my own pace.
The only competition I see is me.
I'm the trainer.
I'm the runner.
I'm the cheering crowd.
I'm the #1 fan.
I'm the winner.
I went the distance.
I uplifted my spirit.

My train of thought can't be stopped.
I'm on my way to the top.
I put in the work and gave myself the credit I deserve.
I never lose.
I only learn.
I stay hungry.
No one can tell me how to run my race.
As long as I'm working on being the best me possible,
As long as I don't let my circumstances define me,
As long as I listen to my intuition,
I will always be in first place.

Coming Up Green

I admire them.
The ones who came from nothing
And turned it into something.
The ones who dare to be themselves.
I admire …
The outcasts,
The weirdos,
The misunderstood,
The doubted,
The underrepresented,
The underdogs,
The visionaries,
The revolutionaries,
The multipotentialites,
The multilayered,
The complicated and complex,
The ones who are slept on, but not for long,
The talented,
The gifted,
The broken,
The hopeless,
The hopeful,
The outspoken,
The soft-spoken,
The open-minded,
The brave,
The bold,
The modest,
The confident,
The fighters,
The survivors.
I've always admired the kids on the come up
With millionaire minds,
Ongoing drive,
And rich souls made of gold

Paper airplanes

Some days I hide.
Some days I confide.
I wish I could travel more.
I tried it once
and thought, *"What am I getting myself into?"*
Is this what it feels like to be daring
Or am I just being scary?
I was afraid to leave
My comfort zone,
Afraid to go up,
To excel.
I forgot to exhale.
I was scared things wouldn't end well.
Mama got me a necklace before my flight.
It had me feeling alright.
Poppin' pills had me feeling alright too.
I know my destination,
But was I destined to make it?
The anxiety—
I couldn't take it,
But I had to fake it,
Just like I always do.
Hey, I think I'm starting to like this view.
There is no turning back.
Don't know what I'm 'bout to do once I get to where I'm going
to.
It's "Fight or flight."
Why fight this feeling? Why run?
Let me take it easy.
Hella breezy.
Glide, get high,
And enjoy the ride.

Air be our God-given substance,
but on the days I can't breathe,
I inhale that God-given tree.

Invisible

I think back to my childhood often. I think back to elementary school. I never truly fit in or had a consistent group of friends. I felt misunderstood often. I was labeled "sensitive" and even "unappreciative."

I think about the imagination I used to have within me; it lifted my spirits. Since then, my mind has shifted like I don't know how to tap into that part of my brain anymore. Like the school system didn't nurture that in us. Every human being is a student of life. We should be encouraged to keep our imagination alive and well. Who are you to tell me to sit down and do the assignment this way, Miss Sallie Mae? Why did we grow up being told that college is the only way? I wish someone would have seen something in me. I wish teachers would have told me I'm special and that my words could take me places. That they could take me anywhere, I wanted to go. That I could be whoever I wanted to be. Why didn't anybody encourage me?

Often, I felt invisible. I might have even been labeled "annoying" in third grade because I wouldn't stop talking in class. I haven't spoken much since then. I remember when wall ball, tetherball, hopscotch, and tag were the things to do on the black top. I remember when wherever my imagination took me was the place to be. I remember when my imagination would follow me.

A child's imagination magnifies the beauty in the here, and now, while an adult's imagination amplifies the fears we place in our minds, fears of the unknown. As children, we used imagination to enrich the present. As adults, we use imagination to create scenarios in our heads about things that haven't happened yet, and often don't happen at all. Why do we waste our energy? Why didn't someone encourage me to keep my dreams in the palm of my hand? Why didn't someone encourage me to dream big? Why didn't someone tell me to enjoy being a kid for as long as I could? Why didn't someone push me into challenging the limits inside my head about who I was and what I was capable of doing? Why didn't someone tell me to be more demanding of the things I say about myself, of the people I surround myself with? Why did it take me twenty-six years to find strength in being resourceful, asking questions, not taking no for an answer, taking leadership, taking risks, seizing opportunities, believing in myself, and finding my voice?

This feeling of losing wasn't my choosing. That makes me very uncomfortable. Pay attention to not only the kids who act out, but also the ones who withdraw. I might be one of the rare breeds who turns my invisibility on and off like a light switch. Some days I want to be seen, some days I want to be heard, some days I just want people to feel me. Other days I'm thankful for my ability to fade into the background.

Willpower

Will I ever get out of this mess?
Will I ever see a day without stress?
Will the people who did me wrong realize the weight of their actions?
Will justice be served?
Will I live to see the day that God seeks vengeance on my behalf?
Will He allow me to witness it?
Will I heal from the things I've witnessed?
Will I stop being the culprit of my own pain?
Will I bring honor to the family name?
Will I make my family proud?
Will I make my city proud?
Will I make my ancestors proud?
Will I see the day that I choose myself first?
Will I find a life partner to satisfy my eternal thirst?
Will I hit rock bottom before I get to the bottom of my issues?

My thoughts about life are different every day. Sometimes it's different every hour. I think God is trying to teach me a lesson and teach me the beauty in willpower.

Kite

I see a way out of this.
I can see the future.
I can see Heaven.
Not in detail,
But I shook hands with Hope.
Destiny was heavy in the air.
Let's not make light of the soul work
And the homework to be done to get there.
I owe nobody an explanation of my destination.
I'm patient.
My body is a home
And I am a homebody.
I face these fears alone.
I hear the wind.
It's God's whisper in physical form.
He says everything is gonna be alright.

Ventilate

Paper cuts on my heart.
Bruises on my brain.
Fire in my lungs.
I don't be feeling the same.
I don't be thinking the same.
I don't be breathing the same.
Some days, I don't even be feeling sane.
This isn't a dirty habit.
It's a desperate cry for revolution.
A war against self.

Unclear

When my mind races, my hands wander
And pick on the parts of me that are too weak to defend themselves.
I bleed out of nervous habit.
Concerns weigh heavy on my mind.
I'm blinded by my own overthinking.
My soul has been seeking peace for years now.
But here I am, still picking myself apart piece by piece
Because I don't know what to do with my hands right now.
This habit of pointing the finger at the person in the mirror
And picking on her
And pointing out every flaw
Is getting out of hand!
I don't understand why I treat myself this way.
I look in the mirror and all I see are scars.
Battle scars on my skin.
Physical manifestations of the battles I fight within.
I give in because ...
Sometimes I'm too tired to fight my thoughts.
Sometimes I'm too weak to break my bad habits.
Sometimes I just need someone to hold my hand.
Someone who will forgive my hands
When I'm too stubborn to.
Someone who understands
That I'm struggling
And doing the best I can.
Someone who can look in my eyes and realize
That these tears are full of uncertainty.
The future is so unclear to me.
And my heart is heavy with fear of never reaching my full potential
Or knowing what it's like to be at peace
Or knowing what it's like to have clear skin.

Beauty marks be my God-given tattoos. I'm still finding meaning in my self-inflicted wounds. I never meant to disrespect His art with my scars.

Hella fly

I'm tryna be hella high.
I'm tryna be hella fly.
I want to fly away.
I want to see the day I get what I prayed for.
I want my dreams to carry me away
On a cloud,
On some loud.
That natural high
That celebratory high
High fives with God.
Proof that I beat the odds
Proof that I ain't no fraud
Proof is in the pudding.
I don't kick it with you 'cause your energy is off-putting.
I think I deserve to feel light
I think I deserve to feel right.
A heavy heart full of spite can't grow wings to fly.
I ...
Forgive you.
Or at least I'm trying to.
I find victory in not letting you get the best of me.
The goal is to let go of all of this baggage.
Badu said it best
You gotta put that shit to rest.
Just when I thought I couldn't get any higher,
Just when I thought my attire couldn't get any flyer,
I remember there are no limits to the things my mind,
body, and soul can do.

Lung (Capacity)

I couldn't breathe today or last night.
I don't remember the last time I felt this way
Like questioning if I'd be okay.
How come it took me this long to learn my panic
Has a name?
That I shouldn't feel ashamed or weird.
That I shouldn't feel like something is wrong with me.
That I can't ask for help or support.
That accommodations are not allowed.

I don't think anyone should be so familiar
With the sensations of a pounding heart,
A mind full of racing thoughts,
Shallow breathing and shallow faith.

I'm starting to think high school days
Were a waste.
The teachers didn't give a shit there.
The teachers simply weren't equipped there.
They only heightened my anxiety.
10,000 hours can be a superpower or a weapon.
My body has spent 10,000 hours being anxious
And I got 10,000 scars to show for it.

I need someone to take my mind and chauffeur it.
I need help with my drive and my state of mind.
I know no mindset can be set in stone
Unless you leave it alone and let it wallow
In its sorrow and toxins.

I need somebody to be my lungs.

I forget to breathe.
I gasp for air at night.
Oxygen is a stranger.
I don't know what my lungs are really capable of.
But they still have the audacity to breathe
With shallow faith.

Breathe. Be.
Believe. Achieve.
Succeed in being free.

Unfamiliarity

Sometime last November, I didn't want to be here anymore. I contemplated what it would feel like not to feel anything anymore. I was trying to be completely selfish for once. People pleasers lose out on the feeling of peace because they never feel good enough. What they do isn't good enough. Who they are isn't true enough.

I was trying to pick up everyone else's broken pieces along with my own. I tried to make a mosaic out of my pain, but it shattered every time I was almost done. Instead, I was walking around on broken glass in the dirt. I questioned whether staying here on Earth would be worth the hurt. But I made sure to keep a smile on my face in public.

In private, I fantasized about taking my last breath. My world was falling apart, so I had nowhere to stand. I was crashing out of the sky with nowhere to land. I had no place in the world, and I didn't feel heard. I thought to myself, What am I doing with my life? God wasted potential on me. I started to believe God isn't as perfect as He seems because he certainly made a mistake making me.

I was too afraid to call anyone for help in my moments of darkness, but I was hoping someone could hear my scream just by looking at my demeanor. I can't moonwalk on water, or else I would. I'd take a rocketship to the moon if I could. I've been through ocean tides, and I survived. I was praying for an out-of-body experience because I didn't want to experience these demons anymore. They were always laughing at me. I didn't want to hurt anymore. It was terrible. Unbearable. The worst pain I've ever felt so far.

But I'm in a better place now. These days I aim to be like water. I want the current to take me farther, like a ripple. I want my resiliency to triple. The truth is, I don't need nobody to save me.

I signed up for swimming lessons last week.

Anti-Summertime

I've been doing a lot of spring cleaning since last summer,
But I can't seem to get rid of this clutter.
I'm unable to utter my feelings,
Because I feel like nobody hears me.
I'm so sick and tired of crying.

I miss my own company,
Because that's when I feel the safest.
Nobody understands me now.
I'm letting everyone down.
I don't know where home is anymore.
It used to be by the poolside
But ...
The sunshine isn't as bright.
The liquor isn't as strong.
The sun doesn't kiss me the same.
Summer anthems are playing in the background,
But all my heart sings are sad songs,
Reminding me of all the things I did wrong.

My happiness never lasts long.
I long for joy
And to fill a void
That summer no longer satisfies.
Hard lemonade leaves a bad taste in my mouth
Reminding me of how hard it was to be lonely
And to be the only one without a reason to celebrate.
The sun used to give me something to believe in,
But I hate summer now.
I hate how I let everyone take the joy out of my favorite season.

What am I supposed to do
with all this loose change?
All I do is exchange my pain for
someone else's insane tendencies.

Shelter

I find myself being home less.
I fantasize about being homeless.
Let me explain.
Let me rephrase.
I can't wait for the day
When I'm brave enough
To make the world my home,
To feel the love everywhere I go.
Moving from state to state,
Meeting people who can relate
And appreciate my art,
Appreciate my heart,
Appreciate my pain.
Meeting people who love me
Even when I'm going insane.

I find myself crashing in the parking lot.
I find myself thinking a lot
About driving far and crashing my car.
Leave me alone.
Let me be.
I look forward to the day I'm free.
To not feel numb anymore,
To not feel sore
From all the emotions I endure.

Moving from state to state,
Meeting souls who can relate
And appreciate my art,
Appreciate my heart,
Appreciate my pain.
Meeting people who love me
Even when I've gone insane.

Open Water

Going inward in open water is my safe place
Yet at the same time
I drown in my quiet space.
I drown in confusion.
I feel guilty for wanting to crawl back into my shell.
It's broken, beaten, and battered,
But I still try to hide and survive
In the mixture of light and darkness.
I am misunderstood by the current waves,
By this current generation,
By those who used to know me best.

This is the first time in my life I started praying for a drought. I'm drowning. Someone get me out.

Place

There's something magical
About visiting a place
You've been before.
Revisiting,
Remembering,
Reminiscing on the beautiful moments
And the hard times.

The last time you stood in this same spot
You were going through a lot.
You were having a mental breakdown.
You were dealing with heartbreak.
You were broken into pieces.
You were searching for peace of mind.
You were having an identity crisis.
You were dealing with drama.
You were dealing with the fact that some things change
And some things stay the same
Including yourself.
Thinking to yourself ...
How do I maintain and keep from going insane?

You were at a place in your life, depressed and stressed
Thinking you were gonna be in this space forever
But when you look at all that you have faced in life so far
You can taste the beauty in the struggle,
In the journey,
In the process.
In the moment, that pain is bitter as hell.
But you're not the same person you were the last time you were
here.
Suddenly, everything tastes sweeter.

Printer

It took every ounce of strength
To get out of bed this morning
And not call in "sick" for work.
It took all my mental power
To convince myself of my self-worth.

I'm convinced I was cursed at birth.
I'm so sensitive.
Everything I touch hurts.

I want to leave this Earth.
I'd be fine if all I left behind were footprints.
Maybe someone else will see them
And finish the blueprint.
No one ever warned me about the fine print.
No one told me it's okay to speak
So I lost my voice.

All this time I thought I was supposed to hide it
And be silent
But now I know better
So I'm trying to find it.

In the meantime
I'll let the ink on this paper
Do the talking for me.
Explore me and get to know more of me
Without interruption.
May it leave an imprint on your soul.

Trying to escape this
emotional jail cell so
I can write well again.

Quicksand

The more we spiral downward
The more my mind spirals out of control.
The more I panic, the more powerless I am.
I don't know how to escape
This quicksand.

I'm 'bout to lose it,
any second now, and
no one would see it coming ...

A Letter to Gigi

Dear inner child,

Forgive me for talking down to you like others do. Forgive me for abandoning you like others did.

Teach me how to be a big kid again. Make me laugh. Give me life. I didn't realize it then, but you're a lot more courageous than I am. I hope who I am and who I'm becoming makes seven-year-old Gianna proud.

I hope you love me. I promise to love you better.

Make time for friends.
Make amends.

Good Morning Text Messages

I miss you.
I miss spending time with you
Because when I spend time with you
I spend time with myself.
I don't need to be in the company of anybody else.
I guess I never really appreciated you before.
It's been a long time since I've seen your bright sunlight smile.
It's been a while since I've been eager to
Feel the chill that you reveal.

I never thought I'd be a morning person.
Every break of dawn, I've been in the habit of breaking bad habits,
But lately, every morning feels like I'm mourning something.
I'm not so quick to get out of bed anymore.
I don't smile anymore.
I don't laugh anymore.
I don't talk anymore,
At least not with sincerity.
I get worried when prayer and poetry no longer bring me an ounce of comfort or clarity.
There's a lot of shit in my head I don't understand right now.
I'm asked to explain myself.
Please don't get mad at me when I can't.
I just want to be alone with you.

Teardrop Tattoo

I can't tell you how many times I've cried
These past few days.
No matter how much or how long I cry
My problems don't fade away.
I cry some more just thinking about it,
Fearing
That my problems are here to stay.
There's nothing like
That cry that's soul-deep,
So deep it reaches the physical part of your instinct
Where your body and spirit are in sync.
That soul cry is your spirit shedding tears,
Shedding fears.
The same way our bodies shed dead skin
And our souls shed dead sin.
The soul sheds pain deep within.
Although I know this to be true,
Sometimes I still have my doubts.
I'm praying that this sadness isn't permanent.

Survival Mode

I'm not a lot of fun right now. Don't confuse my tendency to push you away with me being on the run. I'm not running from shit. If anything, I'm running toward obstacles full force. I was forced into this predicament. I was forced to sacrifice and to clean up a mess that wasn't my own.

Let me be real clear: you don't run shit here. You're not welcome here.

I don't think this is an accurate representation of me. I don't feel like my bubbly self anymore. I'm a lot more serious these days. I'm a lot more intentional with my ways. I don't do shit for fun anymore. I can't afford to.

I can hear my mom say, *"God will reward you."* Note-to-self: *"God will restore you."* If you're trying to get to know me right now, you have to be patient and strong. Otherwise, you and I can't get along. I'm dealing with real-life shit. Some days I can't handle it. I don't have time for someone who doesn't understand me or doesn't try to. This is a bumpy ride. These are heavy times. Every day I work hard to be my own sunshine. Every day I work overtime to keep my family's spirits high. To get to know me is an investment. Your willingness to stick away would be a testament to your ride or die nature. To turn this cold isn't my nature, but things change.

I'm tryna survive. I don't have time to cry. I got people depending on me. This isn't fun and games, homie. You can match my hustle, or you can bounce. When it comes to my life and my heart, get in or get out. But I just want to warn you, here and now...I'm not a lot of fun right now.

pH balance

You can't feel me.
You don't know the real me.
You don't behave.
You wouldn't know how to ride this wave.
You can try, but I won't save you.

I need me a ryde or die.
I need me a brave, fly guy.
A guy who will satisfy
A guy to make my body scream
And my soul cry
And my heart smile
And my mind be sure
That this is love and that we balance each other out
And that we're compatible in every single way.

This might not be something that you're used to.
I don't have patience like I used to.

Behave and ride the wave.
Do as I say.
Give in and let go.
Let me see your breaststroke.
Don't be like those other folks
Who brag and boast.

Are we compatible?
Is this rationale?
Are we just lonely?
Are you the homie?
Can you hold me?

Let me be your favorite body of water.

Go with the Flow

I aim to be like water.
To go with the flow
To hold my shape
To remain current
To flourish
To nourish
To heal
To bless
To give life to anyone
Willing to jump in.
To give props to anyone
Who is without fear to sink or swim.

Transparent.
Flexible.
Resilient.
Life-saving.
Hydrating.

What's the difference?

I need a brand new start.
I need a brand new heart.
I need to feel new again.
If I cry daily, would that be considered
A baptism of holy tears?
Can it wash away all my fears
And the discomfort that change brings?
I don't know what is worse:
When things change, or when they don't.
When people change, or when they won't.
To stay the same, or never change.
Same old, same old.
Different new, different new.

House of Mirrors

I am lost in this house of mirrors.
I don't belong here.
I'm nowhere near finding an open door.
I'm blinded by the sun's glare—
Get me out of here.
Energies and foreign mentalities
Bounce off the walls.
I've had a taste of freedom before.
Love is lost, misery is near ...
I fear there is no way out of here.

All I see is pain
And blame bouncing off the walls
And vaulted ceilings that make me feel so small.

Illusions of space.
Dirty mirrors with unclear intent.
Unfamiliar face.

Physically, there's no space.
Emotionally, I don't feel safe.
I want to leave without a trace.

Clarity

Confusion is my ex.
Delusion is my stalker.
I want to ask Clarity to marry me,
But why even bother?
I am Illusion's daughter.
Reality is not real anymore.
To be real is not the deal anymore.
To heal and be still has never been the drill.
When uncertainty comes knocking at the door,
You know the drill.

People don't see the ripple of their actions.
People can't stand to stand by the still waters.
Why would they bother?
It must be painful to look yourself in the eyes
And realize you don't recognize your own reflection.
It's clear to me that you and I aren't destined.
You haven't learned your lesson.
You haven't made progression.

You have me constantly guessing
If I'm lovable
And if I deserve healing
Or if pain is just the name of the game,
A game I never volunteered to play.

Pollution

Every morning
I used to pour myself a glass of toxins.
Toxic tears, toxic years.
God was getting an earful from me.
Desperate cries,
Burning eyes, stomach churning,
Yearning for death.
Praying it would all end.
Praying for a friend
On days I would look over the edge,
On days when stepping toward the ledge
Sounded so Goddamn peaceful.
To jumpstart my heart
On days I didn't feel a thing.
My heart was giving out.
My mind was giving up.
My veins felt insane.
Pollution.
Intrusion.
I guess I was ruining a good thing.

*Some parts of me are dead,
other parts of me are holding
on for dear life.*

Aftertaste

I have to admit
I'm bitter these days
And there's hate in my heart.
It has me falling apart.
I've been trying to heal for the past two years,
But I don't know where to start.

Lifeguard

Today I noticed I couldn't look at myself in the mirror. I was too shy to look me in the eye. I don't know why. Am I ashamed? Am I dishonest? Is there something I'm not telling myself? Something I'm not paying attention to? I don't recognize that woman in the mirror, but I realize that she deserves my attention, my tough love, my acknowledgment, my acceptance, and my presence. My full attention.

Intention

I'm not gonna act like I'm whole because I'm not. I still have a hole in my heart as I write these words. I've only felt whole once in my whole life thus far, now that I think about it. Feeling whole is a goal of mine, and I know every goal takes time and it takes work.

I have a garden where I plant ideas, grow food for thought, and watch life and death occur. Have you ever heard the question: *Who heals the healer?* With that in mind, I bring flowers to the garden of my soul to mourn the parts of me that have died and celebrate the parts of me that have survived.

People are going to hear what they want to hear and see what they want to see, so I might as well say what I want to say. For the first time in my life, I'm telling myself it's okay to speak up. It's okay to say how I feel. It's okay to state my opinions, thoughts, and concerns. It's okay to disagree. I'm giving my voice permission to be free. I don't have to be loud to be proud. My soft-spoken voice will make its way through the crowd— my way. My whisper can be heard a million miles away. So I'm excited to finally use my words to heal myself. I just want to confess and express that this process of healing is an ongoing adventure.

I didn't realize a little daredevil lives inside of me. She surprises me every once in a while with the decisions she makes and the risks she takes. She's the part of me that's tired of being afraid, tired of being caged by my own destructive beliefs and by toxic people trying to run me out of my own world, trying to throw dirt on my name out of envy, or being petty just because they lack the green thumb.

It's okay. Rub dirt in my wounds and watch my character bloom. There's no more room in my heart for fear. I don't hold onto it anymore—I only need fear, anger, resentment, and pain to push me forward. I wouldn't dare hold the daredevil back. I'm afraid of the things she'll say and the things she'll do if I don't allow her to speak when she asks to. If I don't let her live life the way she wants to. If I don't let her explore. If I continue to ignore her, just to please others and uphold *their* image of me.

I have to admit that I'm still scared to get to the root of my problems, but I do want to solve them. Just like leaves during autumn, I change and I fall ... but just like trees, I still stand tall through it all.

I'm still healing, and that's okay.

Modifications

I found a side of me
I never knew I neglected.
The practice taught me how to be compassionate
Toward a part of me I was embarrassed of.
A part of me I never thought I could improve
Or move with grace.
A part of me I assumed needed saving.
I was disconnected with this side of me.
Backhanded compliments, left and right.

As of now, I can feel the movement.
I stand tall
And stand still with my eyes closed
On top of a mountain.
But I feel my spirit move.
I smile inside
As I realize
I'm doing just fine.
There's nothing wrong with making adjustments.

Naked Garden

I feel my prettiest when these pretty boys leave me alone.
I'm tired of having to change my ringtone
To forget how ugly things got.
I forgot how good it feels to be whole.
I forgot how good it feels to be naked in a room alone,
How good it feels to strip for a party of one,
Strip down to the naked truth,
To enjoy my youth.
My love life is on hold
Until I learn how to hold it together
And find my balance.
It's time to treat myself like royalty
And drink from my chalice.

I feel my sexiest
With no makeup on,
Just a fresh face,
With moisturized lips.
No bra,
And a baggy shirt that hugs my hips.
I love my skin
Dipped in oil.
I spoil myself.
I'm made of honey, honey.
But these fools can't get a damn thing from me.
I don't need your seed in my soil.
I'm done watering dead things.

I feel my best when I tend to my own needs
And when I look like me.

Taste

Time has a lot to do
With the sweetness of life.
The things you once hated
Could become the very things that you love
With time.
Nothing is set in stone.
Tastebuds don't stay the same.
It's okay to change your mind.
It's okay to change over time.

Don't take offense
If you're not someone's cup of tea.
Everyone's palettes are on different levels.
Not everyone has good taste.
But you know what they say about wine ...?
Just give it time.

This Good Earth

I've seen beautiful scenery.
It has taken my breath away.
I know there is way more to see.
This good Earth plants beautiful seeds in my mind.
Flaws bloom into flowers.
The sun and the moon split the hours.
The trees keep me rooted
And inspire me to be as crazy and distorted as I want to be
And to find beauty and growth in my insanity.
They remind me to breathe
And to be still.
The ocean, I respect it
Because it puts life into perspective.
When I have a hard time being in touch within
I listen to the wind.
Waterfalls have shown me the beauty in falling.
O Mother Nature,
I'm on a natural high.
You give me life.

We all have some type of privilege.
We all have something most people don't have. We all have something to be grateful for. Acknowledge it.

Lovely

I've fallen in love with myself before.
I know I can do it again.
For times I was light as a feather,
For times I had the world on my shoulders.
I'm moving mountains and boulders now.
I'm becoming bolder in my way of being.
The older I get, the more I fall in love with my voice.
I let it echo...
I see the light at the end of the tunnel.
I *am* the light at the end of the tunnel.
I see who I am and who I could be.
On a journey to loving myself again.

I'm ready for my blessings
and my blessings are
ready for me.

Lifelong Question

Life is never ending
With lots of pretending
And transcending
And heart mending.
I'm blending sorrows with hallelujahs
To cement, seal, and heal the broken parts of me
That have plenty of stories to tell
And songs to sing
And treasuries to be discovered
And lessons to teach.

I pray for your healing in the
revealing of your heart.
In the depths of your art.
In the end and the start.

Butterflies

Butterflies are angels in disguise.
They come in times of joy and times of distress.
Sometimes they come in times of tests.
When my life is a mess
I know I can look up to them.
They remind me that I am, indeed, one with the universe
And that I have the power to break any curse
Even at my worst,
Even through the hurt,
Even through the bursts of doubt,
Even through anger in large amounts.
They remind me that I will amount to everything.
They remind me that I, too, have wings.

That Glow

I make it a point to
Moisturize,
Visualize,
Memorize,
And conceptualize.
Shades protect my vision.
My skin glistens as I block these shady people.
I daydream about quitting my day job.
I'm in deep thought as I picture paradise.
I deep condition.
My body shows me love when I listen to it.
On a mission to glow from the inside out.

My blessings are already mine.
It's only a matter of time.

Intentions of the Subconscious

He said *I know there's more to you.*
I know you are more than what you go through.
I can't wait to see the day you realize how beautiful you are.
This conversation made me reflect on all of our other
conversations
And it depressed me
To realize that all this time I thought I was being an open book
To the men I've loved and cared about,
To the people I thought deserved it.
I was wrong.
I've never let anyone read past the first couple pages,
But even that is a lot for me to offer.
Everyone always wants to know more.
I let their imagination run wild
In hopes they will be distracted
And forget about the rest of my story,
Their unanswered curiosities,
Their ideas about me.
Some people get mad that they can't read me.
I have everyone exactly where I want them to be,
Unintentionally.

It was never my intention to hurt anyone (else), including myself.

(Recent)er

This is something I've been thinking about recently. I'm slowly learning how to say "no"—and the beauty in it. I don't need a "yes man," and I don't need to be one, either. Sometimes I just need a breather. Honestly, I need them all the time. I need time to recharge and recollect. To reflect and not forget about myself. I'm a person too. I'm an individual. I'm the one to drop everything for everyone. I'm the sunshine when you rain on your own parade, but I need to learn how to save some sunlight for myself.

Fill your own cup first, love.
Make sure you have plenty so
that you're not left empty.

Dig

I picked up a shovel today.
Can't decide if I want to get to the root of my problems
Or dig my own grave.
I'm not very brave these days.
Don't know if I'll ever make it out of here alive.
Don't know if I'll ever heal enough to be real with you.

All the ups and downs, the run arounds. It's all a part of the plan, even if I don't understand.

Simplicity

I'm over "overdoing it."
I'm perfecting imperfection.
Not to mention
I reflected on my reflection in the mirror today
And damn, I look beautiful.
I'm learning to love what I see.
I'm learning to love me.
I hated how I over-exfoliated the frustrated layer of my being
Not seeing I was causing way more damage than I was
preventing.
I was venting and venting and venting
Yet still suffocated due to the lack of ventilation.

I needed a fresh start.
I'm so proud
To stand out from the crowded idea of beauty.
I got lost in the smoke and mirrors.
I felt ugly from the inside out.
I was once a product of my conditioned beliefs.
Removing all my peach fuzz
Made me realize I didn't know who I was.
It's okay to soften up even in a world so hard and cold and
rigid.
Nothing wrong with being shy and timid in my skin.
That's just my way of being humble sometimes
And falling in love with my complexion and curves in silence.

I needed a break from it all, because....
I was having more breakouts than breakthroughs.
I don't need much to feel beautiful now,
I keep it simple.

Mirror: I love you.

Me: I love you too.

Hummingbird

A little bird told me that healing is on the way
That tomorrow will be a brighter day
That the universe will make a way.
She said I would be okay.
She sang me a song to hum along to.
We were in tune.
She pointed to the moon in the morning sky.
She told me that I, too, can fly high.
She told me it's okay to cry
And to not know why.

Most times, healing can't take place
If you misplace your worry,
If you live life in a hurry,
If you don't hum the pain away.
But a little bird told me everything will be okay.

Unity

The world can be scary
The world can be cold,
But we all need love
No matter how young or old.
Let's come together
While the world falls apart.
Let's remind the world
People still have a heart.

Flower Power

    I'm depending on flower power to get me through the hour. I've been walking around with a sour taste in my month. Don't know up from down. Don't know my way around town. Things are different now. Craving the feeling of being safe and sound. I sound confused, safe to say. I got sirens going off in my head everyday. I used to refuse the idea of blowing trees, but tree be the thing that got me feeling free lately.

Daisies

Aiming to have clear skin
And clear intentions.
I look at my wounds in the mirror
And I wonder how we got here.
I pray to God that my wounds are rich enough to plant daisies in them.
I want to see a healed inner child rise to the surface.
She deserves to make an appearance.
I want to heal her from every trigger.

Who heals the healer?

116

X-ray

To heal is to feel
And reveal every bit of brokenness
Within so you can quit going without.
So you can quit living in doubt.
So you can take the route toward joy.

I got trust issues in my muscle tissue,
Feverous rage in my ribcage,
And icicles in my heart chambers.
What am I to do now?
There's no one to help me out
So I've been having conversations with the God within
And the daredevil within.
Both want me to win.

B.S.

Back on my bullshit.
My soul is translucent.
I came from the dirt.
Down to Earth.
You don't know my worth.
You don't know my hurt.
You ain't ever had a love like this before.
The type of love that keeps you coming back for more.
I keep it running.
I hope you've been working on your sidestep.
I'm the loyal kind.
I'm one of a kind.
I'm a dying breed.
Feed my senses
Or end up in the trenches.

Moving in Silence

I'm still shy, timid, reserved, quiet, whatever you want to call it—but inside me, you would witness a riot. I'm constantly fighting the pressure I put on myself to be someone or something other than me, other than G, other than myself. I have to remind myself not to shy away from the fact that I am powerful. I know how to speak up softly but with sincerity—with the goal of bringing clarity. My quietness makes them scared of me. I'm still learning how to be a leader. I'm still learning how to voice my perspective without convincing myself no one cares about what I have to say. At least I shared and dared to let my thoughts kiss the universe.

Waiting, achieving, and receiving.
Patience, preparation,
and perceiving.
Faith, trust, and believing.

Sandcastle

I'm still learning the beauty of letting things go.
I become so attached to things and people I love that
When things fall apart, so do I.
It's important to start building myself up
And be proud of what I have built
And to go with the flow.
To stay current
And in the moment.
It's beautiful to watch things melt away and become one with
everything that is
Rather than watching it crash down into flames.
I'm trying to change the way I see things.
I am the queen of the castle.
Constantly reinventing myself
With curiosity and creativity.

Light Years

I need to embrace this stardust. I'm tryna develop a lust for reaching my higher self, for reaching a higher source—because self-love is a must, of course. I pray to the stars, *Am I on the right course? Have I not shown enough remorse? Have I not shown enough compassion toward myself? Do I hate me?* I have many questions, but one thing I won't question is existence. I won't argue with distance. I won't fight with resistance. I hope to learn how to find peace in an instant.

Will I master it in this lifetime, or will I find myself light years away from the purest part of my being? Will I lose track of time? Only I can learn the ins and outs of who I am. Only I am aware of my superpowers and doubts. Inner space is the place to be. There you will see the wonder, curiosity, discovery, and God-given treasures waiting to be unlocked.

Inner space.

There's a lot that takes place here, like meditation, insight, memories, and reflection. Letting my guard down takes place here. Letting go takes place here. Letting God in takes place here. Peace holds space here. Safety holds space here. Loved ones hold space here. Silent noise holds space here. Forgiveness holds space here. This space holds peace of mind, pieces of the moon and sky, especially the moments when they gracefully collide. This is not a place to hide. This is a place to simply be because when you're free, you don't need to hide. This space holds stillness.

I'm still unwrapping this gift of free will. It kills me to have so much freedom and no structure. I blame it on my perfectionism, but maybe that's the point. Maybe I need to muster up the courage to set things free and let them be. Let things be what they are. Let people be who they are without judgment or an urge to fix without getting in the mix. I think we all want to feel something. I think we all want to reveal something. I think we all want an experience of a lifetime, but we are the experience; we are the existence. We can choose to run *from* or run to ourselves. My goal is to master my soul and be one with everything and everyone around me. We are all one. We share time and space together. We may experience different storms, different weather, but we're all in this together—whether we like it or not.

Why not learn from one another? How much time will it take to realize all we ever needed was each other?

Give Me Space

I look up at the sky as the stars align. I'm hoping to connect the dots. I pray to God, hoping He will help me collect my thoughts. Doing so, so I feel less lost.

Does dreaming come with a cost? I earned a college degree and everyone is so proud of me, but the enemy keeps telling me that I'll never succeed. I'm scared and unprepared, unaware of myself while everyone else seems so sure of themselves. Everyone else seems so put together while I'm fighting internal storms and depressing weather.

Give me space.
Give me room.
Give me time.

Window(s)

A lot of people think they know me.
They don't know what they're talking about.
I barely know myself.

I've built a wall.
It's the only thing that makes me feel tall.
It's the only way I keep from falling.
No one has the patience to knock on the door of my heart,
Never mind forgiving me when I'm too afraid to answer.
They see the wall, but they forget about the windows.
They don't care about these windows.
They see a wall, and they want to tear it down.

I can see right through their bullshit.
If I entertain it, it's only because I'm bored.
At the end of the day, I close the blinds for two windows
Just to get away from it all,
But the third window is never blind.

Keep your distance.
Respect my existence.

Headspace

Nobody can see me crawling back into my shell.
Nobody knows me well enough to see me withdrawing into
the dark,
Letting my mind visit some scary places.
Nobody sees me, but that's okay.
No one gets me
And I get it.
I probably look unfamiliar,
Unrecognizable.
Somewhat the same, but somewhat different.
I shouldn't be punished or judged for trying to figure it all out.
I'm not trying to take my uncertainty out on anyone.
That's why I stay silent.
That's why I prefer to be alone.
I don't like when people try to force their way into my world,
Uninvited.

I don't know how much more withdrawn I could be,
But it's starting to feel crowded in here
Even when it's just me.

How long will it take me?
I see other people do it.
I see other people fluent in
the language of their soul.

Orbit

I'm learning to remain still when my mind is spinning. It's not about stopping the madness; it's about organized chaos. I release my thoughts and let them float away. I let them come and go without judgment. I don't force them to leave. I don't rush it. God gave me a mind to think. So why waste it, chase it, or make it strive for perfection? There's no such thing. I'm going in circles. I'm going insane, as I will always remain unless I abstain from putting shame on my brain for trying to connect the dots. For trying to find its way. For trying to find its place in space.

The God Within

The other day I woke up with one hand on my heart and the
other on my stomach.
My soul was making sure I was breathing and that my heart
was still beating.
I guess I do care.
I guess I still want to be here.
I have unfinished business.
I have so much life left to live,
God willing.
Every morning I have been waking up with a heavy chest and
no appetite.
But that night, my spirit was comforting me in my sleep.
I woke up at peace.
The God within me still loves me

Take caution when ...
Taking risks
Taking advice
Taking advantage
Taking drugs
Taking time
Will it throw you in or out
of your divine timeline?

Staring at Starry Nights

I stare off into space.
I don't recognize this place
Called Earth anymore.
We live in a different world now.
In a world of our own.
No wonder we're alone.
What have we become, other than selfish?
Lost ...
We've lost our mind.
We've lost our sense of compassion.
We've lost our sense of self.
We're confused.
Every other day is bad news.

I'm somewhere between
Wishing I could save the planet
And wishing I could get the hell up out of here.
I wish I could live on the moon
So I can love the world from a distance,
But here I am, still
Fantasizing about joy, adventure, freedom,
And peace of mind
As I stare off into space.

Spaced out

I keep my enemies spaced out.
Some of them are "spaced out"
Without a doubt.
Spaced out in different amounts,
But who's keeping count?
Keep your distance.
Respect my existence.
Listen to my leisure.
Never been a deceiver.
Always been a firm believer
In the beauty of distance and space
And the time it takes
To come to a mutual agreement,
To come to a mutual respect.
I expect my enemies
To find a remedy for their envy
Or get left with no regret
On my end ... "friend."

Out of body.
Out of place.
Outer space.

135

Sensations

Someone asked me how I was feeling today.
I said, "I feel good."
They said, "How do you know?"
I said, "What do you mean?"
They said, "How do you know you feel good? What does feeling good *feel* like?"
I responded, "I feel light and warm. My scars are no longer sore. My heartbeat is steady and ready to make a comeback from the setbacks of unfortunate events. I feel no regrets and smell incenses full of insight. And when I check the state of my mind, I find my thoughts aren't in competition with each other. That's how I know I feel good today."

The God Within II

God is my intuition,
But I didn't listen.
I miss Him.
Why do I ignore what He has given me?
I've always known that God is within me.

This is the first time in my life I've felt abandoned by everyone
... including Him.
Are my prayers being heard?
What are You trying to teach me?
Am I blocking my own blessings?
Is that why You can't reach me?
Release me from the chains of fear, hopelessness, and doubt.
I'm not familiar with the distance
And silence between us.
I'm out of touch with You and myself.
Lord, I need Your help.

I watched God and the angels
play pool with the planets.
They have it all mapped out.
So why should I have any doubt?

Galaxy

She is not from here.
Not from this atmosphere.
Not from this side of town.
But I'm sure you'll see her around.
You will see her in every lover,
You will see her in every tree,
You will see her in every window
And in every melody.
That might sound absurd,
But you heard it here first.
You will see her in the night sky.
You will see her in different lifetimes.

Her ways might seem strange
To the simple-minded,
But she is a simple being, simply being
With complexity in her energy.
She is a remedy.
She is a frequency.
She is a galaxy.

Gifted

You can't rid what is God-given.
I'm living with a gift.
Have I disappointed the Anointed One
With the ways I use it
Or the days I refuse it?
Do I ever abuse it?
They say if you don't use it, you lose it.
Is there truth to that?
Will my youth come back
If I tap into that gift?
Will my gift allow me to dream and drift?
To cope?
To float with hope?
I don't take this gift as a joke.
I'm quite honored.
Thank you Father.

Meteor Showers

When it rains, it pours.
The damage leaves a sore spot.
I've experienced too much invasion,
But I'm trading resentment for forgiveness.
I'm not 'bout to carry all of this with me.
It's not mine to carry.
It's scary to let go of the only feeling you know.
The only feeling that seems to give you strength in a world so
fake.
When it rains, it pours.
But I've been through this before.
Time and time again.
I won't hold on to this damage anymore.

Hold yourself accountable
when you ...
Hold grudges
Hold yourself back
Hold someone else back
Hold conversations with a fool
Hold your tongue at the wrong times

Strive to hold space instead.

Wholesome

Be selective of who you let in, not only into your world but into your space, because space is a different place. If I let you in my world, you're here in the physical, you're in front of my face—but if I allow you in my space, you forever hold a place in my heart. I carry you within my spirit. I've allowed you to see my ugliest flaws, trusting that you'd see the miracle in them. When it comes to who you let in, make room and make way for only what is wholesome.

Queen of the (Soul)ar System

I am plenty.
I forgive myself.
I am whole.
I know when to let go.
I know when to hold on.
I am strong.
I am out of this world.
I am timeless.
I'm a diamond.
I am reminded.
I am guided.
I am not alone.
I am with self.
I am home.
I have arrived.

I am a simple being,
simply being

Cosm(et)ic

This is my attempt to personify
The night sky
And how the stars beautifully
Mark her dark skin.
He counts each and every one of them
And knows them all by heart.
She is his moon, sun, and world.
His favorite girl.
She is earthy and moves mountains
With her ocean tides.
Her beauty marks are his favorite parts
(of her exterior).
He counts them to calm his worries.
He reads them like a map.
A cosmic story.

Godspeed (Poetry In Motion)

You can never say I was heartless.
As a matter of fact, you should be astonished
By the way I work hard and I love hard.
If we fell off it's 'cause you couldn't keep up.
My only wish is that you would wish me well
Because I don't have time to wait.
I don't have time to waste.
Things don't always go my way, but…
God makes no mistakes
Or mishaps.

Perhaps you're unfamiliar with the fact
That I've been through hell and back
Time and time again.
And the thing about time is…it's perfect.
And perfect timing is not mine.
It's perfect because perfect timing is divine.

There's nothing that no one can tell me
No obstacle that can derail me.
Because I'm moving at God speed.
I'm a product of ambition and faith.

Making a way out of no way
Is how we do it over here.

Night Sky

I'm not asking for an apology.
I'm not asking for your approval.
I'm not asking for your opinion.
I'm not asking for the world.
I'm only asking for space.
Give me space.
Give me time
To connect with my divine.
I'm tryna connect the dots
With a finger tracing the night sky
And my eyes on the prize.
I still get surprised when I watch the stars align
With God's will for me.
I'm tryna be lowkey
So I don't ruin what He has in store for me.

Besides God,
The night sky knows me best.
She doesn't make light of my pain during my darkest hours.

Astronaut

Imagine me in a spacesuit.
Freedom suits me well
If you couldn't tell.
I've put in the work to soothe my soul.
I have no limits.
The sky is my ally.
My dreams take me sky high.

I like this view.
The journey and hard work was all worth it.
I'm glad I didn't give up.
I'm glad I didn't give in.
You gotta stay true to the mission.
You got to listen
To the stars and the planets.
All this time you thought you had to plan it
But everything is already established.
You just got to manage, and take nothing for granted.
What is yours is already yours.
Don't ignore the tour
If you're tryna soar,
If you're tryna live more.

Them: "It's just a phase."

Me: "Don't judge my lunar cycles."

Neptune

They can kill me,
But they can't take my soul.
They can't take my inner peace.
They can't contain the energy I release.
I am continuous.
I expand.
I demand that my presence
Be noticed, in the most humble way.
You can't take what is not yours.
I am a being.
My only job is to be.
I have no start or end.

Don't pretend you don't see the galaxy within me.
I see it in me.
I see it in you.
It's our job to be in tune
No matter the distance.

Everyone deserves a space to be their true authentic self. It's everyone's responsibility to create those safe spaces. Everyone is out of this world. So no one should feel out of place.

Household

I am home.
I have arrived.
I thrive in every setting.
Here, there is no pretending.
Here, there is no judgment.
Here, there is no fear.
Only love
And peace
And release
And being.

Just be.
Just be here.
Just be near.
Just be clear
About who you are,
About how you love,
About how you arrive.

Welcome home.

Acknowledgments

I want to start by giving a huge thank you to *you,* the reader. Thank you, any and everyone who has ever supported my poetry by giving me feedback, encouraging me to never stop writing, being a part of my launch team, and simply taking time out of your day to read my work. Every single one of you played a part in building me up and turning my hobby into a dream of becoming a published author. Shout out to Stephanie for the beautiful interior illustrations. Thank you for blessing this project with your talent. Special shout out to my best friend and favorite photographer, Diane, for taking my author photo and for always providing love and support. Thank you for believing in me.

Thank you, Mom, for teaching me the beauty of words and the power they hold in their definitions. The day you told me how proud you were after hearing my piece at a virtual open mic night meant the world to me. More than you'll ever know. It gave me the push I needed to not give up on this project and to always write from the heart without fear. To my little sisters, Gia and Jasmine, I love you so much. You inspire me every day with your creativity, intelligence, and big hearts. Always stay true to who you are, what you believe in, and what makes you happy. Shout out to my brother Lee. I wouldn't have been able to finish this book in a timely manner without you. I became an official writer when you helped me build my desk. Thank you for playing a part in my journey.

To everyone at Self Publishing School (SPS), thank you for all the support and resources that have helped make this dream a reality. Without this community, I still would have been overwhelmed and unmotivated to finish this book. Thank you, Chandler, for your YouTube channel and webinars. Your enthusiasm got me excited about writing again and gave me hope. Thank you, Dillion, for being such a joy to speak with and for believing in my vision. To my coaches, Ramy and Barbara, thank you for your words of wisdom, for answering all of my questions, and guiding me with encouragement and honesty. Special shout out to my accountability partner and fellow author, Liza, AKA Full Moon. Our weekly phone calls made me feel like I wasn't going through this process alone. Your energy is beautiful, and your accountability was exactly what I needed when I was starting to feel discouraged. To the whole SPS community, thank you for welcoming me with open arms.

Thank you, God, for blessing me with the gift of words. Thank you for answering my prayers and taking my heart's desire into consideration. You've always had my back.

About the Author

Gianna Baldazo

In and Out of My Element is Baldazo's first published book. This book has helped her find her voice ... and she has plenty more to say. Follow her on social media for more poetry and updates on future projects.

Instagram: @giannabaldazo